Creative History

Valerie Evans

Acknowledgements

The author and publishers would like to thank Peter Kellie, Sue Butcher and the staff at Little Ealing Primary School for their support whilst working on this book.

Thanks also to the creative children at Little Ealing Primary School who have contributed their work to this book, demonstrating their many talents and their versatility.

Finally, a big thank you to Maurice, Suzannah and Grace Evans, Edith Markham and Laura Harman for their contributions.

Egyptian Jewellery Boxes (page 11)

Published by Collins, An imprint of HarperCollins*Publishers*
77 – 85 Fulham Palace Road, Hammersmith, London, W6 8JB

Browse the complete Collins catalogue at
www.collinseducation.com

© HarperCollins*Publishers* Limited 2011
Previously published in 2004 by Folens
First published in 2004 by Belair Publications

10 9 8 7 6 5 4 3 2 1

ISBN-13 978-0-00-743950-8

Valerie Evans asserts her moral rights to be identified as the author of this work

British Library Cataloguing in Publication Data
A Catalogue record for this publication is available from the British Library

Every effort has been made to trace copyright holders and to obtain their permission for the use of copyright material. The authors and publishers will gladly receive any information enabling them to rectify any error or omission in subsequent editions.

Commissioning Editor: Zoë Nichols
Cover design: Mount Deluxe
Photography: Kelvin Freeman

Editors: Emma Thomas/Jill Adam
Page Layout: Patricia Hollingsworth
Illustrations: Page 16 and 66: Sara Silcock; Page 72: Celia Hart

Printed and bound by Printing Express Limited, Hong Kong

Contents

Introduction

How people lived in ancient times – the clothes they wore, the food they ate, the homes they lived in – have had an effect on the way we live today. History is full of fascinating facts and information, which can inspire our creativity. This book introduces eight cultures of the past – Ancient Egyptian, Aztec, Ancient Greek, Roman, Native American, Australian Aborigine, Ancient Indian and Viking. Within each chapter the children explore different elements of these cultures such as: beliefs and legends, ceremonies and rituals, clothing and jewellery, transport, food and how people used to live.

The aim of this book is to teach history in a fun and practical way, using art activities linked to a theme. Each theme begins with a useful paragraph explaining key facts and providing introductory ideas to inspire your pupils. The activities use art materials in new ways to produce whole class and smaller tabletop displays related to the history project.

The activities in the book can be used in two ways – to enhance an existing class history project or as stand-alone mini art projects with a historical focus.

Give your class a change from drawing and painting on paper! This book enables pupils to experiment with different materials such as sandpaper, aluminium foil, modroc and clay.

Each chapter includes small and larger scale projects in 2-D and 3-D. Art is about having fun, learning and trying new techniques. Encourage the children to interpret their ideas in different ways and to suggest alternative methods and materials, where appropriate, to achieve the desired effect.

I hope the ideas in this book will inspire your children and demonstrate how history can be taught alongside art in an engaging way using the simplest of materials available in schools.

Enjoy learning about history in a creative way.

Valerie Evans

Beliefs

The Ancient Egyptians firmly believed in an afterlife and prepared carefully for it, burying their dead with food, belongings and even servants for the long journey ahead. The body of a dead person would go through a process called mummification. The intestines, stomach, liver and lungs would be removed from the body and stored in Canopic jars. After a drying process, the body would be packed with linen, sawdust and spices and wrapped in linen bandages. Often spells were written on the bandages and then the mummy would be placed in a coffin made from stone, clay or wood. The mummy was then placed in a tomb – the most grand and elaborate of these being the Pharaohs' pyramids.

© Corel

Create an Egyptian tomb in one corner of the classroom with a life-sized wax batik mummy, clay Canopic jars and painted plaster plaques for the tomb walls.

Wax Batik Mummy

Resources
- Roll of white paper
- Wax crayons
- Selection of different coloured drawing inks
- Paintbrushes
- Iron and white sugar paper

Approach

1. Draw around a child with their arms folded on their chest and their legs together to make the shape of a mummy.

2. Decorate the mummy with vibrant Egyptian designs and hieroglyphs, pressing heavily with the wax crayons to make a bold design.

3. Cut out the mummy.

4. Carefully screw up the mummy into a tight ball, taking care not to tear the paper, and then flatten it out.

5. Paint over different parts of the design with different coloured drawing inks and allow it to dry.

6. Iron the mummy between sheets of clean white sugar paper and add it to the display.

 Note: An adult should use the iron at all times.

Canopic Jars

The organs of the dead were preserved and placed in containers called Canopic jars. The jars had lids in the shape of the heads of four Egyptian gods. The baboon-headed jar contained the lungs; the falcon guarded the intestines; the jackal looked after the stomach and the human-headed jar held the liver. These jars were buried with the body.

Resources
- Clay and clay tools
- Slip
- Paints and paintbrushes
- Varnish

Approach

1. Roll a small ball of clay and flatten it to make the base of each Canopic jar.

2. Make a small thumb pot from a ball of clay and fill it with water so there is a continuous supply of slip for joining the clay.

3. Make the jar using coils of clay and join using a clay tool so that the jar has a smooth finish.

4. Model the human, jackal, baboon and falcon heads for the lids of the Canopic jars. Attach the ears, noses and beaks with slip from the thumb pot. Use different clay tools to give the impression of hair, fur and feathers on the different creatures.

5. Add a cylinder of clay to the base of each lid as a stopper.

6. Paint the jars with hieroglyphs in a strip down the front of each jar. Varnish the jars when dry.

Tomb Wall Plaques

Plasterers covered the tomb walls with a smooth surface ready for decoration. The walls were marked out in squares corresponding to a grid on the design for the tomb wall. The walls of the tombs of ordinary people would be decorated with scenes of people at work or at rest in the realm of Osiris. Royal tomb walls would often show the myth of Re and scenes of the dead person's future life. An assistant made the paints by grinding minerals to powder on a block with a stone. Water, gum or egg white would be added to make the paints.

Resources
- Plaster of Paris
- Sturdy shoebox lids
- Powder paints, paintbrushes, white chalk, charcoal sticks
- Eggs

Approach

1. Make plaster plaques. Mix the plaster of Paris as directed and pour it into sturdy shoebox lids.

2. Leave to harden for 20 minutes.

3. Mix paints using powder paints and water. Make white from ground chalk and egg white and black from ground charcoal sticks and egg white, as the Egyptians would have done.

   ⚠ **Note**: Some children are allergic to egg white, so check with parents or carers for any allergies. As an alternative to using egg white, mix black and white powder paint.

4. Sketch out a tomb wall design in pencil.

5. Remove the hardened plaque from the cardboard lid and paint the design.

6. Display with the batik mummy case and the Canopic jars in the class Egyptian tomb.

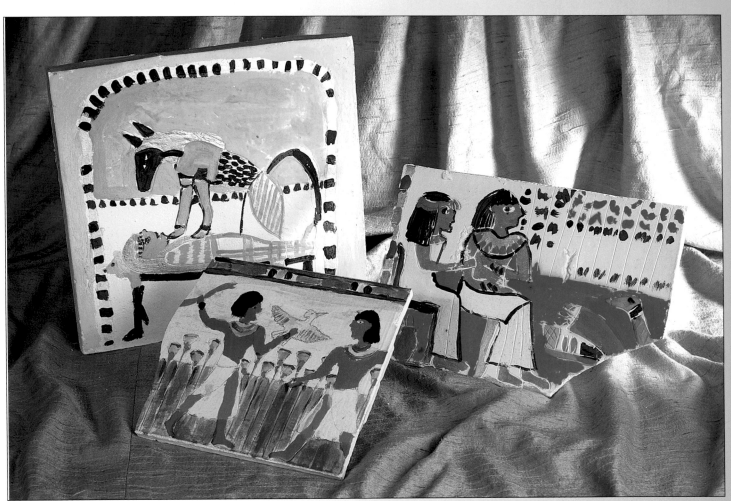

Gods

The Ancient Egyptians had gods for every aspect of life and the afterlife. Some of these gods partially took the form of animals and many were related. Anubis, the god who protected the tombs of the dead, had a jackal's head; Bast, the goddess of love and joy, was a cat; Hathor, the goddess of music and love, was shown in the form of a cow and Sobek had a crocodile's head. Although the gods Osiris and Isis had a human form, their son, Horus, was the falcon-headed god.

Egyptian Chess Set

Research the gods and goddesses of Ancient Egypt. Design a chess set modelling eight of the animal-headed gods from clay. Make clay pyramids to replace the pawns in a chess game.

Approach

1. Make sketches of the gods and goddesses to be used in the chess set. Eight animal-headed gods in Ancient Egypt were Re, Bes, Amun-Re, Osiris, Isis, Horus, Anubis and Seth. Cats were also very important to the Ancient Egyptians.

2. Model the different gods, placing them all on thrones so that the figures are seated. Remember to create two versions of each god, one for each colour. If modelling cats, add gold wire around the neck and through one of the ears and jewels or sequins for the eyes.

Resources
- Clay and clay tools
- Paints, varnish and paintbrushes
- Gold picture wire
- Felt and softboard
- Sequins or jewels
- Glue or sewing needles and thread

3. Shape eight identical pyramids for each side, adding texture by using the different clay tools.

4. Paint the pieces in two different colours and varnish them when dry.

5. Cut out felt squares in two colours and sew or glue onto a large piece of softboard.

Legends

Legends tell us that the Egyptian Universe began in water and darkness. Atum, the first sun god, gave birth to twins – Shu, who represented the air and Tefnut, who was the goddess of water. They, in turn, had twins called Nut and Geb. It was Nut, the sky goddess, who stretched her star-covered body across the world. Geb's body formed the earth and Shu's strong arms stopped the heavens collapsing on those below.

The Egyptians believed that they would live on in the stars in the Next World. Many coffin lids were decorated with paintings of Nut stretching across the universe with her beautiful star-covered body.

Circular Story of Nut and Geb

Resources
- Large plastic hoop
- Watercolour pencils and paintbrushes
- White sugar paper
- Green shiny paper
- Starry wrapping paper
- Wool or string
- Gold and silver gummed stars
- Sticky tape

Approach

1. Put the plastic hoop on a large piece of white sugar paper and draw around the circle.

2. Draw Shu standing in the middle of the paper with Nut stretched out across the sky and Geb lying below Shu.

3. Cut the shape of Nut out of starry wrapping paper and Geb from green shiny paper.

4. Colour the picture using watercolour pencils.

5. With a paintbrush and water, wash over the pencil to give the impression of a painted watercolour.

6. Glue the starry Nut to the top of the picture and attach green Geb at the bottom.

7. Hang different lengths of string from the bottom of the hoop and add gummed stars to them.

8. When the painting is dry tape it to the hoop. Hang the hoop from the classroom ceiling with string.

Clothing, Jewellery and Make-up

The Ancient Egyptians wore skirts, dresses and robes made from white linen. Both men and women wore make-up and jewellery. Lip and eye paints were made from minerals, which were ground into powder and then mixed with oil or water. Fine brushes and sticks were used to apply the make-up. Cheeks were painted with red clay (ochre) mixed with water, and henna was used to redden palms and the soles of feet.

Because of the hot climate, most Egyptians wore their hair short. When more elaborate styles were required, ornaments were added to heavy wigs of curls and plaits made from real hair. Young girls often wore their hair in plaits and boys shaved their heads leaving a single lock of hair hanging down.

Dough Heads

Approach

Resources
- Plain flour and salt
- Mixing bowl and spoon
- Aluminium foil
- Non-stick baking tray
- Paints, varnish and paintbrushes
- Wool and black felt

1. Make up salt dough using a mixture of two cups of flour to every cup of salt used.

2. Add water to the mixture until it makes a soft, pliable dough – not too dry and not too sticky.

3. Model a flat Egyptian head and shoulders from a hand-sized ball of dough. Add a nose and ears, fixing them to the head with water. Press into the dough to create lips and eye sockets.

4. Use a pencil to make holes in the ears for earrings.

5. Place the back of the face over a large ball of aluminium foil to give it a rounded, three-dimensional shape. Put the model onto a non-stick baking tray and bake in the oven at 150°C (300°F, Gas Mark 2) for 3–4 hours. Leave the dough models to cool in the oven.

6. Paint the faces. Add 'eyeshadow' (in paint) to the women's faces before varnishing them.

7. Add hair made from wool in plaits or black felt for short hair.

Egyptian Jewellery Boxes

Many Ancient Egyptians wore wide bead collars decorated with coral and turquoise and fastened by cords at the back of the neck. Most jewellery was decorated with charms, such as the scarab beetle or the eye of the god Horus, to ward off evil spirits. Large pendants, called pectorals were worn as well as string necklaces, bracelets, armlets and anklets. The jewellery would be kept in decorated boxes or baskets.

Resources
- Wire and pliers or string
- Beads, jewels, pasta
- Cardboard
- Glue
- Shoeboxes
- 3-D paints, gold spray paint
- Masking tape

Approach

1. Draw designs for the jewellery using pictures and posters of Egyptian artwork for ideas.

2. Cut out cardboard earrings, headdresses and pectorals and then glue on a mixture of gold-sprayed pasta shapes, beads and jewels.

3. Thread beads onto wire or string. Tape the pendants and pectorals to the bead strings and attach them to the dough models made in the activity on page 10.

4. Attach wire to the earrings and thread them through the holes in the dough models' ears.

5. To create the jewellery box, paint a shoebox or other cardboard box one colour and then add Egyptian designs and patterns using 3-D paints.

Buildings and Transport

We have a good idea about how the Ancient Egyptians lived from 'soul houses', which were pottery models of homes put into tombs in preparation for the afterlife. Everyone lived in homes made from mudbricks. The windows were set high in the walls to keep the rooms inside as cool as possible. Ordinary houses had mudbrick shelves instead of beds and only a few chairs or tables. Wealthy people had large, beautifully decorated homes – often with gardens and pools. The walls were painted in bright colours with leather wall hangings and rugs hung on display. Temples were built along the banks of the Nile, each one dedicated to the worship of a particular god or goddess.

Dough Homes

Make a model showing houses built along the banks of the Nile with different kinds of Egyptian boats on the river.

Approach

1. Apply a wash of water to the background sugar paper. Then add red and orange paint to make a sunset sky. Sprinkle on some salt for a textured, grainy effect.

2. Print some palm tree trunks onto the background using fingerprints and paint the tops of the palm trees.

3. In the mixing bowl, make up a salt dough mixture with two cups of flour to every cup of salt used. Add water slowly to make a pliable dough.

4. Roll out the dough on a floured surface and use clay tools to cut out different shaped buildings. Use clay tools to press and cut out the shapes of windows and doors in the houses.

Resources
- Plain flour and salt
- Mixing bowl and spoon
- Paints, varnish and paintbrushes
- Large sheet of white sugar paper
- Glue
- Large sheet of shiny blue paper
- Rolling pins and clay tools
- Non-stick baking tray

5. Put the dough houses onto a non-stick baking tray and bake in the oven at 150°C (300°F, Gas Mark 2) for 3–4 hours. Leave them in the oven to cool.

6. Paint and varnish the houses. Glue them to the sunset background.

7. Use the shiny blue paper to create a river in front of the homes.

Funeral Barge

Embalmers used funeral barges to carry dead bodies across the Nile to their workshops. Sometimes model boats would be placed in tombs to represent the boat that carried dead people across the Nile to the Next World.

Resources
- Clay and clay tools
- Wooden sticks
- Rectangular pieces of leather or cotton fabric
- Cardboard
- Glue
- Paints, varnish and paintbrushes

Approach

1. Model the funeral barge in clay with a coffin shape on a raised platform above the deck.

2. Embed four sticks into the clay to hold the fabric canopy over the body, then allow the clay to dry.

3. Paint the funeral barge.

4. Glue on the fabric canopy. Oars can be made from sticks and cardboard.

5. Varnish the boat.

Papyrus Boat

Papyrus boats were the main form of transport in Ancient Egypt. They were used to transport goods across the Nile and as fishing and bird-hunting vessels.

Resources
- Straw
- Corrugated cardboard
- String
- Clay and clay tools
- Paints and paintbrushes
- Glue and varnish

Approach

1. Tie the straw into bundles with string. Bind the bundles together onto a piece of corrugated cardboard cut in the shape of a simple boat.

2. Make apples, onions, pomegranates and cucumbers from clay. Paint the fruit and vegetables, and varnish when dry.

3. Glue the fruit onto the boat and display with the funeral barge.

Childhood, Toys and Games

Children in Ancient Egypt played with brightly-coloured balls stuffed with feathers. Tomb paintings show children playing ball games whilst riding piggyback. They also played leapfrog and tug-of-war. Their toys included spinning tops, dolls and model animals made from mud or wood. In the board game 'Serpent', the board was shaped like a coiled snake. Players threw coloured balls and moved lion-shaped pieces to reach the snake's head in the middle. Board games were so popular with both young and old that they were placed in burial tombs for the person to play in the next life.

Serpent Game

Approach

1. Take a ball of clay and roll it into a sausage shape. Use two hands to shape it into a long coil, working from the centre outwards to keep the coil an even thickness.

2. Starting at the centre, transform the coil into a snake by flattening the end of the sausage and raising it above the coils.

3. On the reverse side of the snake join the coils with a suitable clay tool.

4. Mark sections along the snake by scoring with a clay tool at regular intervals.

5. Add eyes and patterning to the head and raised part of the snake.

6. When the clay is dry, paint and varnish the board or cover it with brown shoe polish and rub it with a duster until it shines.

7. Play the game with plastic counters or make the traditional lion counters from clay. Use a dice to determine the number of moves or devise your own rules.

Resources
- Clay and clay tools
- Paints and paintbrushes
- Varnish
- Brown shoe polish, cloth and duster

Food

Grain was the most important crop in Ancient Egypt. It was used to make bread and beer, which were consumed daily. Wealthy people enjoyed beef, duck, goose, goat and a variety of fish but the poor mainly ate vegetables such as beans, leeks, onions, cabbage and turnips. Salads of lettuce and cucumber were popular. A meal would often end with fruit, nuts, cakes or pastries. Honey was used to sweeten foods.

Egyptian Bowls

Food was eaten from beautifully decorated bowls and dishes made from faïence – a glassy pottery. The most popular colour for this pottery was turquoise. Poorer people ate from plain pottery. People ate with their fingers; no spoons or forks were used.

Approach

1. Cover the outside of the bowl with petroleum jelly to use as a mould.

2. Mix the paste following the manufacturer's instructions and add newspaper strips to the bowl, building up five or six layers. Leave to dry, then remove from the mould.

3. Add a final layer of turquoise and blue tissue paper to both the inside and outside of your bowl.

4. When dry, add an Egyptian design to your bowl using a black felt-tipped pen.

5. Paste small paper plates with torn pieces of blue and turquoise tissue paper and allow them to dry.

6. Add an Egyptian design to the plates and incorporate them in a display with the bowls.

Resources
- Large bowl
- Petroleum jelly
- Newspaper strips
- Cellulose paste powder and water
- Turquoise and blue tissue paper
- Black felt-tipped pens
- Small paper plates

15

Beliefs

In Aztec mythology there had been four earlier periods of history, each destroyed by a different catastrophic event. The Aztecs believed their world, the fifth, would be wiped out by earthquakes and that human sacrifices were necessary for the sun to rise every day. Very few examples of Aztec scripts (codices) are still in existence because many of their documents were burned during the Conquest. Despite the rudimentary nature of their writing system, it is believed that the Aztecs produced manuscripts on subjects as diverse as timekeeping, astronomy and astrology, mythology and history. The writing system consisted of a series of pictorial symbols called glyphs, which were commonly used in the two Aztec calendars (seasonal and religious). The 20 glyphs used to describe the days in the Aztec's religious calendar can be seen on this page. These glyphs were also symbols of familiar everyday objects.

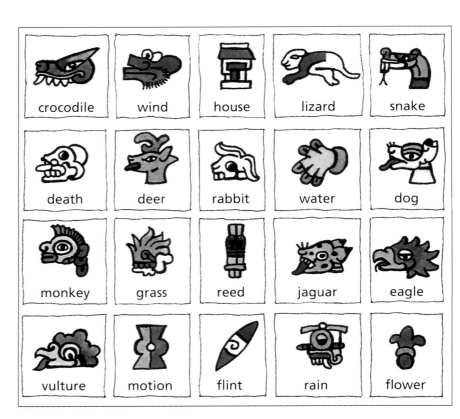

crocodile	wind	house	lizard	snake
death	deer	rabbit	water	dog
monkey	grass	reed	jaguar	eagle
vulture	motion	flint	rain	flower

Glyph Printing Blocks

Resources
- Wooden blocks or offcuts
- Coloured foam
- PVA glue
- Paints and paintbrushes
- Ballpoint pens
- Paper

Approach

1. Design a glyph on coloured foam with a ballpoint pen.

2. Cut out the shape and glue it to one of the wooden blocks. Leave it to dry.

3. Use a paintbrush to apply the paint to the foam and then print onto paper to make a border for Aztec written work.

Calendar Stones

The Aztecs had more than 1600 gods that they believed watched over them and protected them. They believed that the gods shed blood to create their world and that they should repay this by making animal and human sacrifices to them.

The Aztecs used calendar stones to mark the passage of time. They believed that time was like a wheel, endlessly turning. On their religious ritual calendar stone, each day had a name (of which there were 20) and a number up to 13. The Aztec seasonal calendar had 18 months of 20 days with five unlucky extra days adding up to a year of 365 days. The Aztec sun god, Tonatiuh, is depicted at the centre of a huge seasonal calendar stone, measuring nearly four metres across, that was found in Mexico City. His tongue hangs out of his mouth showing his thirst for blood. The stone also depicts the four failed suns (of the previous mythological eras), symbols of the religious calendar and two large fire serpents that were a symbol of time.

Research the gods of the Aztecs and look at pictures of real calendar stones. Design and make a calendar stone from clay.

Approach

Resources
- Clay and clay tools
- Brown shoe polish
- Cloth and duster

1. Mould small stamps from clay showing the Aztec picture symbols called glyphs. Shape handles on the back of the stamps to allow for easy use.

2. Make stamps for the five suns and the fire serpents.

3. Allow the stamps to dry and harden.

4. Make a large disc of clay and press the stamps into the soft clay to create an authentic design. Allow the disc to dry and harden.

5. Cover the 'stone' with brown shoe polish working it into the design with a cloth and then polish it with a duster.

6. Display the calendar stone with the clay stamps.

Gods and Temples

The Aztecs had a god for every aspect of human life. Huitzilopochtli the tribal god, also known as the Hummingbird, led the gods and constantly demanded sacrifices from the Aztecs. The Aztecs built temples to him and many other gods. Every home had its own little altar and small shrines displaying statues of gods but at festival times everyone would worship together in the temple. Sacrifices took place outside temples at the top of the steep staircases where everybody could witness the event. The priests sacrificed thousands of people in the belief that this would keep the gods happy and stop them from destroying the world.

Aztec Knife Handles

Resources
- Clay and clay tools
- Fimo and rolling pins
- Pieces of blunt slate or wood
- Paints, varnish and paintbrushes

Approach

1. Roll out the Fimo, then cut it into small squares. Bake them in the oven as directed on the packet.

2. Make sketches for the designs of the knife handles.

3. Model the shape of a knife handle in clay and push a piece of blunt slate or wood into the finished handle as the blade.

4. Push Fimo squares into the soft clay of the handle to make the design.

5. Allow the handle to harden, then it can be painted and varnished.

⚠ **Note**: Make sure the children understand that even blunt objects can be dangerous if not handled carefully.

Gods and Goddesses

Coatlicue the earth goddess was depicted wearing a skirt of writhing serpents with a heart and skull hung around her neck. She represented the pain of life and was there to remind the Aztecs that they too would return to the Earth. Tlaloc was the god of water and rain. The Aztecs thought that they would starve if Tlaloc was not kept happy and so there were many festivals held throughout the year to pray for rain. At this festival there would be dancing, feasting and sacrifices made to the god himself.

Tezcatlipoca was the giver and taker of life – the god of magic, war and death. He was always in conflict with Quetzalcoatl the god of creation, learning and holiness. Together they represented both sides of human nature. Quetzalcoatl was a feathered serpent adorned with the beautiful feathers from the quetzal bird. Tezcatlipoca can be identified by his missing foot, which was eaten by an earth monster as he dragged the world from the waters before all human life.

Look at pictures of the Aztec gods and make models to depict them.

Resources
- Modelling wire and pliers
- Newspaper
- Masking tape
- Modroc plaster bandages
- Pipe cleaners
- Feathers
- Paints and paintbrushes

Approach

1. Make the body framework of the chosen god with wire.

2. Fold newspaper sheets repeatedly into narrow strips fixed at both ends with masking tape.

3. Wind the newspaper strips around the wire framework to shape the body and fix in place with masking tape.

4. Cut strips of modroc, soak as directed for 3–4 seconds, and cover the body framework. Leave to dry and harden.

5. Paint the Aztec gods using bright colours.

6. Add details such as pipe cleaners for the writhing serpents on the skirt of Coatlicue or feathers in the headdress of Quetzalcoatl, to make the gods distinctive.

Clothing and Jewellery

An Aztec's clothing and hairstyle showed his or her wealth and status and it was an offence to wear the incorrect clothing. Ordinary people wore a loincloth and a plain white cloak made from the magney plant (cactus fibre). Nobles could wear decorated cotton cloaks to below the knee and elaborate headdresses. Women wore plain wrap-around skirts and decorated ponchos. Some nobles wore more than one cloak to show off their wealth. Young men shaved their heads leaving a pigtail, which would only be cut after success in battle. Women often plaited their hair or wore it in bunches with a braided headband. Aztec nobles wore an amazing variety of jewellery including earrings, lip pendants and nose and earplugs. Gold and silver jewellery and masks would be worn on special ceremonial days. The Aztecs used turquoise, obsidian, jade, pearls and shells in their jewellery.

Peg-doll Aztecs

Resources
- Round-headed pegs
- White cotton fabric
- Wool
- Feathers and jewels
- Paints and paintbrushes
- Fabric crayons

Approach

1. Paint the heads and legs of the peg-doll Aztecs adding make-up and jewellery.

2. Add wool for the hair showing the different Aztec styles.

3. Make skirts, cloaks and ponchos from the white cotton material adding details with fabric crayons, feathers and jewels.

4. Display the dolls in social groups.

Aztec Headdresses

The Aztecs excelled in feather work, making elaborate plumed headdresses for emperors and the Aztec nobility. Feather work was a major Aztec industry. Headdresses were made with the feathers of birds such as the heron and turkey and the brilliantly-coloured feathers of the quetzal. The quetzal was sacred to the Aztecs and once the feathers were plucked from the bird it would be released.

Resources
- Large plastic hoops
- Papier-mâché pulp
- Feathers
- String and masking tape
- Jewels, beads and pasta
- Wool, ribbons, pipe cleaners
- Paints and paintbrushes
- Cardboard, paper plates

Approach

1. Add papier-mâché pulp to a card head and shoulders cut-out to create an Aztec bust. Alternatively, paint features onto a face made from card.

2. Stick feathers into the papier-mâché while it is moist and make holes in the ears with a pencil.

3. Allow the heads to harden and then paint them.

4. Add earrings and necklaces made from the pasta, beads and jewels to the Aztec head.

5. Cut triangular notches around paper plates and wind wool around each plate to create a loom framework for weaving. Weave ribbons, wool and pipe cleaners through the 'loom'. Staple the plates to the model heads and attach large feathers to complete the headdresses.

6. Attach the models to plastic hoops with masking tape and hang up to display.

Aztec Masks

Aztecs often wore masks during ritual dances and religious ceremonies such as animal and human sacrifices. Masks allowed the wearer to transform from human form into a spiritual being. Masks were often made as offerings to the gods who were also depicted wearing them.

Resources
- Clay and clay tools
- Fimo
- Rolling pins
- Broken shells
- Paints and paintbrushes
- Varnish

Approach

1. Roll out the Fimo and then cut it into small squares. Bake the Fimo in the oven following the instructions on the packet.

2. Model a facemask in clay, adding a nose and cutting out holes for the eyes. Add white Fimo squares or use pieces of broken shell for the teeth.

3. Use the small, coloured Fimo squares to decorate the mask and leave it to harden.

4. Paint the mask in vibrant colours and varnish when it is dry.

Childhood and Toys

Great celebrations followed the birth of an Aztec baby, often lasting for days. Astrologers would find the most suitable day for the baby to be named. Growing up, the baby would play with rattles and pottery toys that could be pulled along on wheels.

Aztec children were taught at home and learned the skills they would need as adults. Boys were taught fishing and woodwork until the age of eight when some would go to school to learn to be warriors or priests. Girls were taught cooking, spinning and weaving and would marry at about 16 years of age, ready to have as many children as possible. Some girls attended school and went on to become priestesses or healers.

Clay Toys

Research the toys that Aztec children might have played with. Design your own clay toys.

Approach

Resources
- Terracotta or other clay
- Clay tools
- String
- Wheels and axles
- Paints and paintbrushes
- Varnish

1. Make designs in a sketchbook listing the materials that will be needed. The toy could be on wheels so that it can be pulled along. Alternatively, the children could choose to make a rattle.

2. Model the toy from clay, using clay tools to make patterned designs as well as for joining.

3. Attach the wheels to the clay as best suits the design.

4. Paint and varnish the models when they have hardened. Terracotta clay can be left unpainted so the natural red clay can be appreciated.

The Aztec Army

The Aztecs were fierce warriors and neighbouring tribes feared them. The commanders and knights wore grand, colourful uniforms with different feathers showing the rank of the soldier. Eagle knights wore eagle's head helmets in battle and the Jaguar knights the skins of jaguars. Warriors carried shields made from wood and leather and decorated with feathers.

Resources

- Cardboard discs or polystyrene pizza bases
- Roll of white paper
- Wooden dowelling
- Paints and paintbrushes
- Feathers
- Glue
- White A4 paper
- Black wax crayons
- Aluminium foil

Aztec Warriors

Create a large class collage showing Aztec warriors going into battle.

Approach

1. Ask several children to lie on their sides on white paper and draw around them. They should hold up one arm as if holding a spear.

2. Draw eagle's head helmets on two of the warriors.

3. Paint the figures in colourful Aztec costumes.

4. Alternatively, draw a jaguar-skin pattern on white paper with black wax crayon and paint over it with a watered-down yellow paint wash. Use this animal-print paper to add 'jaguar skins' to some of the warriors.

5. Cover the cardboard discs with aluminium foil that has been scrunched up gently and then flattened. Paint an Aztec design on the foil shields and decorate them with coloured feathers.

6. Create spears from dowelling and use cardboard for tips.

7. Glue the shields and spears onto the warriors to complete the collage.

Aztec Shields

The Aztecs used brightly-coloured feathers to make beautiful shields. Aztec kings, nobles and warriors carried them on special occasions. Green feathers from the quetzal bird and bright blue feathers from the hummingbird were popular adornments to the shields.

Resources
- A brightly-coloured feather duster
- Large cardboard discs
- Gold and silver outliner pens
- Glue

Approach

Make a display of shields following the instructions on page 24 (see **5**) or using the method below.

1. Draw a design onto a cardboard disc with a pencil.

2. Go over the design with gold or silver outliner pens.

3. Pull the feathers out of the feather duster. (This is by far the cheapest way to buy feathers in bulk.)

4. Glue the feathers onto the shield taking care not to cover the gold and silver design.

Beliefs

The Ancient Greeks believed that their gods watched over them all the time, their power made evident by the clash of lightning or the howling of a strong wind. They believed the gods looked like themselves and felt human emotions but were immortal with magical powers. The Greeks offered small sacrifices to the gods in the hope that they would protect them from all misfortunes.

The Ancient Greeks painted beautiful vases showing scenes from everyday life, gods, myths and legends. Black-figure vase painting began around 700 BC and was followed by red-figure painting 200 years later. Vases often showed several Greek gods, musicians and dancers.

Greek Vases

Approach

Resources
- Terracotta pots
- Black paint
- Paintbrushes
- Varnish

1. Using a pencil, draw different Greek gods and goddesses or illustrate a Greek legend around the pot.

2. Either paint the figures black or paint around the outlines of the figures in black leaving the figures the terracotta colour of the pot.

3. Varnish the pots when the paint has dried.

Funeral Rites

When a Greek died his or her body was washed, sprinkled with herbs and perfumed oil and dressed in clean, white clothes leaving the face uncovered. Sometimes jewellery, such as a pottery necklace, was made especially to decorate the dead body. Greek legend tells how Charon, a ghostly ferryman, rowed the dead across the River Styx which was the boundary between the worlds of the living and the dead. A silver coin was placed in the dead person's mouth to pay Charon.

Pottery Necklaces

Resources
- Terracotta or other clay
- Wire and pliers
- Clay tools
- Gold paint
- Paintbrushes

Approach

1. Roll eight small balls of clay and then flatten them into discs.

2. Thread the discs onto a length of wire.

3. Decorate each disc using a variety of clay tools.

4. Make eight small, flat pot shapes and decorate them with clay tool markings.

5. Use pliers to cut some wire into eight lengths of 3cm each.

6. Attach the pots to the discs by pushing the wires through the discs and the pots.

7. Allow the necklace to dry and harden, then paint it gold. The terracotta necklace can be left unpainted, so the natural red clay can be appreciated.

Legends

Greek mythology is full of wonderful stories of heroes overcoming encounters with terrible and unusual monsters. Medusa was a female gorgon with a horrific face and hair full of snakes. Those who looked at her were turned into stone until the hero Perseus was able to behead her using a magic shield in which he could only see her reflection.

Medusa's Head

Read the stories of Medusa and create large pictures of her head.

Resources

- Plain flour and salt
- Mixing bowl and spoon
- Clay tools
- Large sheets of white or brown cardboard
- Paints, paintbrushes and PVA glue
- Sequins and jewels
- Silver tape

Approach

1. Ask a small group of children to draw and paint Medusa's head with frightening, staring, fiery eyes.

2. Make up salt dough using a mixture of two cups of flour to every cup of salt used and then stir in water to make a pliable consistency.

3. Roll small pieces of dough into snake shapes. Add patterns and eyes using clay tools.

4. Bake the snakes in the oven at 150°C (300°F, Gas Mark 2) for 1–2 hours and leave them to cool in the oven.

5. Paint the snakes in bright colours. Once the paint is dry, add a coat of PVA glue as a varnish.

6. Glue the snakes onto the picture as Medusa's hair.

7. Add jewels to Medusa's staring eyes and glue sequins onto the snakes. Use silver tape to make a picture frame.

Odysseus and the Cyclops

The adventures of the mythical hero Odysseus are well known. At one point on his journey, Odysseus and his men are trapped in a cave by a carnivorous one-eyed giant; a Cyclops called Polyphemus. Odysseus eventually stabs the giant in his eye with a red-hot stake, blinding him. They escape from the cave clinging to the undersides of sheep.

Make clay models to tell this part of the story.

Resources
- Clay and clay tools
- Large bead
- Garlic press
- Rolling pins
- Paints and paintbrushes
- White pipe cleaners
- Varnish
- Pebbles
- Thin stick

Approach

1. From a rectangular piece of clay, model a cave shape adding a few pebbles to the soft clay at the bottom.

2. Model the Cyclops and join to the cave.

3. Push a large bead into the Cyclops' forehead as his single eye and push a thin stick through his hand before leaving the model to harden.

4. Model some sheep and rams in clay. Push clay through a garlic press and use these strands for their wool. Push curled white pipe cleaners into the rams' heads as horns.

5. Model the body of Odysseus and some of his men and join underneath the body of the sheep using clay tools. Leave the models to harden.

6. Paint and varnish all the models and display as shown.

Music and Entertainment

Music and dance were very important in Greek life, particularly at religious ceremonies, family celebrations and dramatic performances. Musicians were often female. The flute, lyre, timpanon, drums, cymbals and pipes known as auloi were the most popular instruments. The timpanon was a tambourine made from animal skin stretched over a frame.

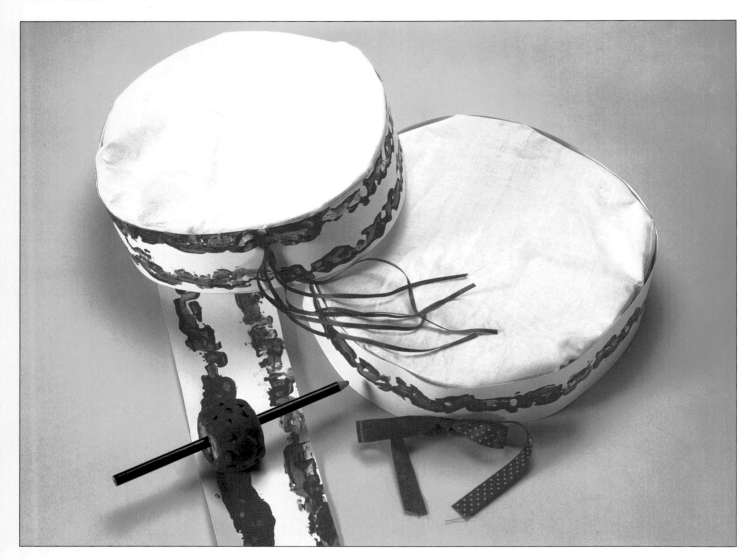

Timpanons

Approach

Resources
- Cream calico fabric
- Strips of stiff cardboard
- Plasticine and clay tools
- Cotton reels
- Stapler and staples
- Paints, paint trays and paintbrushes
- Ribbons

1. Wrap a strip of plasticine around a cotton reel. Press a clay tool into the plasticine to make an Ancient Greek design.

2. Push a pencil through the hole in the cotton reel.

3. Roll the cotton reel in paint and then roll it along the strip of stiff cardboard so it prints a continuous design.

4. Bend another strip of cardboard into a hoop and staple the ends together.

5. Cut the calico into a circle slightly larger than the hoop, stretch it over the hoop and staple it down.

6. Staple the decorated cardboard strip over the first hoop to complete the timpanon. Add ribbon as a finishing touch.

Theatre

Every major Greek city had an open-air theatre. Greek men loved to go to the theatre where they would watch male actors taking on the roles of both men and women as only men could take part in Greek drama. People often went to the theatre for the whole day to watch a variety of tragic and comic plays. Masks would help the actors portray whether the character was male or female, young or old, beautiful or ugly. The actors would often wear elaborate, colourful costumes, wigs and raised platform shoes.

Greek Masks

Resources
- Thin cardboard
- Modroc plaster bandages
- String
- Glue
- Paints and paintbrushes

Approach

1. Make masks from thin cardboard with eyeholes and exaggerated mouth holes. Cut and staple the chin to shape it.

2. Soak strips of modroc in water for a few seconds as directed on the packet and cover the masks.

3. Glue on straight and coiled lengths of string for hair and beards.

4. Allow the masks to dry and harden, then paint them to show different characters.

Sport and Fitness

The Ancient Greeks thought that their bodies should be strong and healthy and they loved sport. Races were run to honour the gods and this led to the first Olympic Games. The Games were held at Olympia every four years and all wars between Greek cities were suspended while the Games were in progress. The Games included running races, wrestling, chariot racing, the long jump, the pentathlon and throwing the discus and the javelin. Athletes competed naked apart from helmets and greaves (leg-guards). In one race they would run in armour and were required to carry a heavy shield.

Greek Shield

Resources
- Thick cardboard
- Aluminium foil
- Paints and paintbrushes

Approach

1. Cut out a large circular shape from cardboard.
2. Tear off a sheet of aluminium foil that is slightly larger than the cardboard and scrunch it up gently.
3. Flatten out the aluminium foil and cover the cardboard circle with it.
4. Paint a Grecian design on the shield and display it.

Greek Helmet

Resources
- Balloon, pot
- White card, masking tape
- Modroc plaster bandages
- Bronze or gold paint and paintbrushes
- Four small scrubbing brushes and glue

Approach

1. Blow up and tie a balloon and balance it in a pot.
2. Cut a rectangular piece of card and tape around the bottom half of the balloon using strips of masking tape to keep it in place.
3. After soaking the strips of modroc for a few seconds, build a helmet shape of 2–3 layers, with guards along the cheeks and a bridge above the nose. Make sure some strips overlap the card and the balloon to make the helmet more secure. Allow the modroc to dry and harden.
4. Paint the helmet with bronze or gold paint and glue on four small scrubbing brushes to form a plume.

Health and Medicine

The Greeks would try to cure diseases in a number of ways. They might pray to Asclepius, the god of healing, or visit a doctor. If they believed Asclepius had cured them they would hang the shape of the healed body part on the wall of their temple as an offer of thanksgiving. A doctor would look at all aspects of a person's life to try to find the cause of a medical problem – perhaps prescribing a medicine made from plants or performing a simple operation if necessary.

Temple Wall Plaque

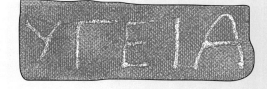

Resources
- Clay
- Plaster of Paris
- Glue
- Paints and paintbrushes
- Cardboard box lids
- Hardboard

Approach

1. Make a rectangle of clay that fits into a box lid.

2. Press a child's hand or foot into the clay to make an imprint.

3. Pour in plaster of Paris and leave to harden.

4. Tear away the box lid and lift the plaque from the clay. Paint the plaque.

5. Glue the plaque to a piece of hardboard. Add Greek words and symbols to decorate.

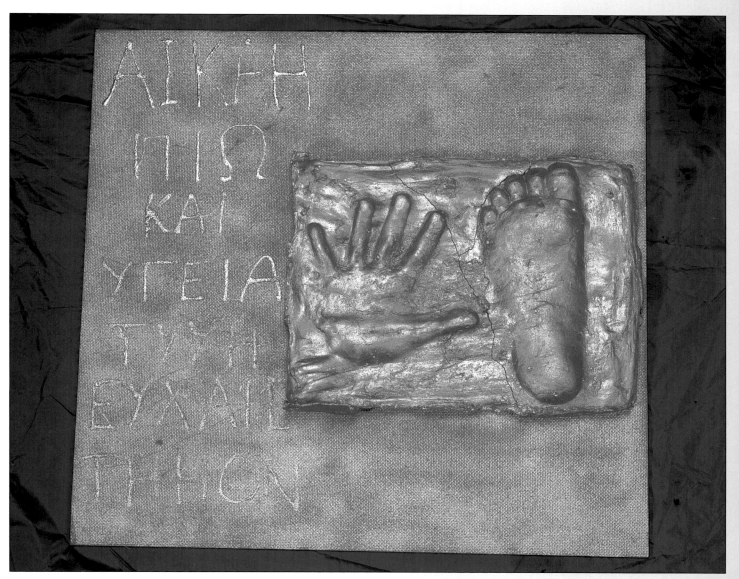

Beliefs

The Romans believed in many gods and goddesses and they tried hard to please them so that they would have good luck in return. They built temples for the gods and were quite superstitious, believing that the gods sent signs to show their displeasure. Special priests called augurs were meant to explain what these signs meant.

In early Roman times it was customary to mint coins depicting Roman gods. The later Romans were more likely to show monuments and the head of the current emperor on their coins.

Roman Coins

Design some coins depicting the Roman gods. Make one coin showing the god Janus with two heads – one looking back to the past and one looking forward to the future.

Resources
- Gold spray paint
- Cardboard discs or paper plates
- PVA or UHU glue
- Aluminium foil
- Black and gold paint, paintbrushes

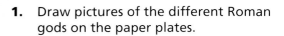

Approach

1. Draw pictures of the different Roman gods on the paper plates.

2. Use a very fine paintbrush to go over the design with glue.

3. Allow the glue to dry and harden.

4. Spray the plates with gold paint to show a raised outline of the Roman god.

5. To create the effect of a tarnished, old Roman coin, crumple foil gently and then flatten it to wrap around a paper plate.

6. Spray or dab gold paint over the foil. Paint the god and an inscription in black to finish the coin.

The Romulus and Remus Legend

A legend tells of the twins Romulus and Remus who were cast adrift in a wicker basket on the River Tiber by their wicked uncle. Instead of drowning, the twins were rescued by a she-wolf who suckled the babies and kept them alive. The royal shepherd took the boys in, after discovering that they were the sons of Mars, the god of war. They went on to found the town that was to become the city of Rome. Both boys wanted to be king of the town and a fight led to the death of Remus. Romulus became the first king of Rome in 753 BC, giving it his name.

Make a sculpture showing the she-wolf suckling Romulus and Remus.

Resources
- Small plastic water bottle
- Piece of wood for the base of the sculpture
- Papier-mâché pulp
- Black paint and paintbrushes
- Four sticks of wood

Approach

1. Make up a mixture of papier-mâché pulp.

2. Cover the plastic bottle with the pulp, shaping a wolf's head at one end. Allow the pulp to harden slightly.

3. Cover the wooden base with papier-mâché pulp and embed the four wooden sticks as the wolf's legs.

4. Put the body on the legs and continue covering with papier-mâché pulp. Allow the papier-mâché to dry and harden.

5. Model the two children, Romulus and Remus, in sitting positions and then join onto the base – one fitting under the wolf and one to the side.

6. When the model is dry, paint it all over with black paint.

Clothing and Jewellery

Nearly all Romans wore tunics that were loose fitting and comfortable for the hot Mediterranean climate. Men in Ancient Rome would wear a toga over their tunics and ladies would wear a dress known as a stole over theirs. Make-up was fashionable in Roman times. Women used chalk powder or white lead for a fair complexion adding rouge to the cheeks and lips. Hair was curled, plaited or pinned up and held in place with a comb according to the fashion of the time. Both men and women were quite fastidious about their appearance and would use a mirror to check how they looked. As mirror glass was not available, the Romans made mirrors with highly polished pieces of silver or bronze that were beautifully engraved on the back.

Roman Mirrors

Resources

- Foil baking trays
- Ballpoint pens
- Stapler and staples
- Aluminium foil
- White sugar paper
- Paints and paintbrushes
- Fabric

Approach

1. Using a ballpoint pen, draw a design on the base of a foil baking tray pressing hard with the pen.

2. Turn the foil tray over so that the raised embossed side is visible and staple on a handle, also made from foil.

3. Draw around two children on white sugar paper. Paint and dress the figures as a Roman man and woman.

4. Display the mirrors around the two cut-out figures.

Cameos, Bracelets and Rings

All Romans wore jewellery. The rich wore gold and silver necklaces and bracelets whilst bronze was a cheaper substitute for the less wealthy. Rings were popular for men and women in Roman times. They were decorated with amber, emeralds or pearls. Engaged couples exchanged gold rings often showing clasped hands, which symbolized marriage. Miniature carvings in semi-precious stone, called cameos, were also popular. They were made from rocks with different coloured layers. They were sometimes worn as brooches and medallions. Many cameos showed portraits of famous people.

Resources
- Beige, brown and yellow plasticine
- Clay tools
- Small jewels

Approach

1. Make an oval of beige plasticine and slice it into layers with a pointed clay tool.

2. Make a second oval of plasticine in brown and repeat as above.

3. Using a pointed clay tool, draw and cut out the profile of a famous Roman emperor from one of the pieces of brown plasticine.

4. Make a cameo brooch by joining different coloured layers of plasticine and adding the profile to the top.

5. Model marriage rings in yellow plasticine and make snake shapes to bend into bracelets.

6. Add a design of clasped hands to the top of the rings and decorate the bracelets with jewels.

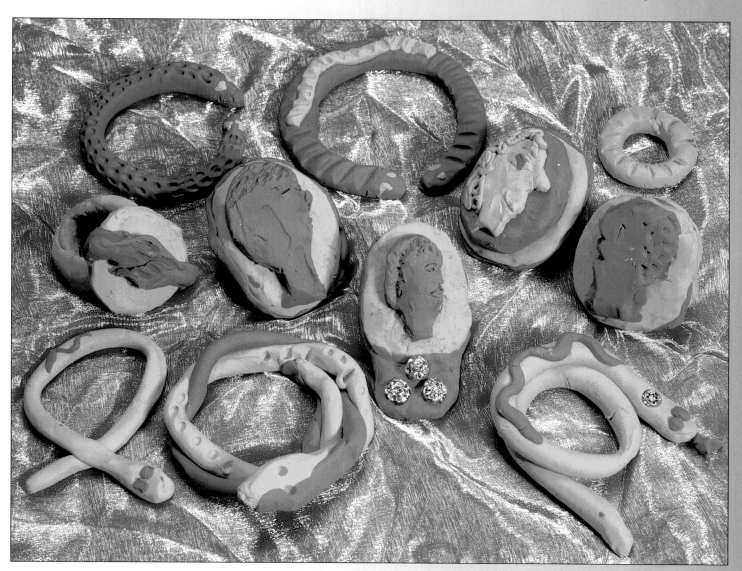

Buildings and Interiors

Rich and poor Romans lived very different lives in very different homes. Peasants in the country lived in simple dwellings made from interwoven branches packed with mud under thatched roofs. Wealthy people lived in towns or in country villas. Their houses were built out of brick and tiles and their windows had glass in them. The walls were covered with plaster and had patterns and pictures painted on them. They even painted on the ceilings in some houses. They had separate kitchens, dining rooms, bedrooms and bathrooms, all with underfloor heating. Mosaic pavements and floors were popular in Roman times. Sea creatures were very common mosaic designs.

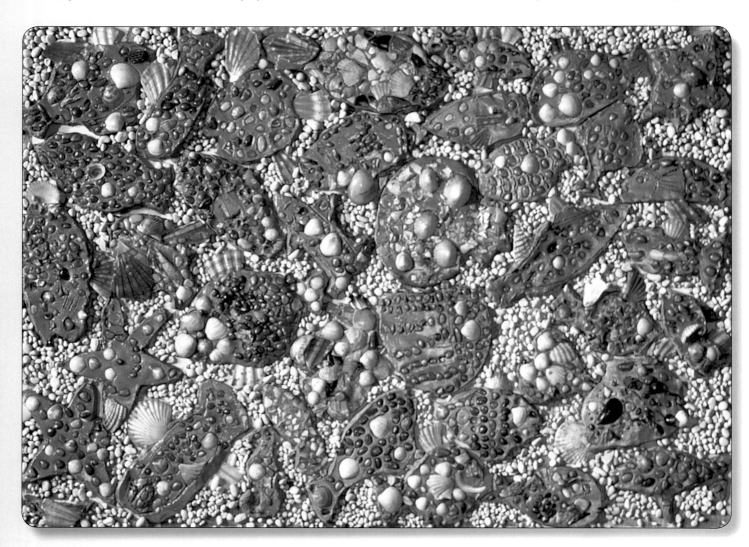

Sea Creature Shell Mosaic

Resources
- Clay and clay tools
- Rolling pins
- Small pebbles
- Shells
- Plywood
- Glue
- Varnish

Approach

1. Roll out the clay to approximately 2cm in thickness.

2. Use a clay tool to draw the outline of a fish, eel or octopus onto the clay and cut it out.

3. Press pebbles and whole or broken shells into the clay.

4. Allow the clay to harden and then varnish.

5. Glue all the individual sea creatures onto one large piece of plywood to make a class mosaic. Fill in the gaps with small pebbles.

Furniture

Wealthy Romans used tables, chairs and stools in their homes but they usually slept on mattresses rather than beds. They lay on couches to eat their main meal of the day. A Roman stool was called a scamnum. Four-legged stools had a square or rectangular top and were often made of bronze. Stools with round wooden tops had three legs.

Approach

1. Tape different shaped boxes together with masking tape to make basic couches, stools and chairs.

2. Soak strips of modroc for 3–4 seconds as directed on the packet and cover each piece of furniture with 2–3 layers of modroc. Leave to dry and harden.

3. Paint the furniture.

4. Cut pieces of foam to fit the top of stools and the seating for the chairs and couches.

5. Arranging the furniture on a painted mosaic floor creates an effective display.

Resources
- Assortment of boxes
- Cardboard tubes
- Masking tape
- Modroc plaster bandages
- Paints and paintbrushes
- Sponge foam

Still-life Painting

Wealthy Romans loved to have the ceilings and walls in their houses covered with paintings and intricate patterns. Artists would be hired to produce small panel paintings, many of them showing a still life. They would be displayed on a wall or on an easel.

Resources

- Paints and paintbrushes
- Calico fabric
- Selection of different-sized box lids
- Stapler and staples
- Still-life subjects such as pots, bowls, apples, grapes and so on
- Thick cardboard and glue
- Shells and gold or silver spray paint
- Small easels

Approach

1. Set up a still-life display, like the one shown in the photo, with apples and grapes in a bowl or pot.

2. Make a sketch of the still life in pencil on a piece of calico fabric cut slightly larger than the box lid.

3. Staple the fabric over the sides of the box lid so that the material is taut.

4. Paint the still life.

5. Create picture frames from thick cardboard decorated with shells.

6. Spray the picture frames silver or gold and display the still-life paintings in them on small easels.

Food

There was a wide variety of food on offer for wealthy Romans who would eat a long, leisurely meal in the late afternoon. A meal might begin with eggs, snails or shellfish followed by meat in a highly-flavoured sauce. Dessert would be cake or fruit and the meal would be washed down with wine, beer or mead. Bread would be eaten at most meals and the Romans would eat with their fingers. They enjoyed entertaining friends at banquets. Guests lay on couches to eat and were waited on by slaves. Poorer people would eat a staple diet of bread, porridge and vegetables such as carrots, cabbage, parsnips and celery. Historians have learned a great deal about how the Romans cooked from recipes collected by a man called Apicius over 2000 years ago. Archaeologists have also discovered the remains of utensils the Romans used when cooking.

Roman Cookery Book

Research the recipes that Romans are reported to have used to make a class cookery book.

Resources
- White card
- Mosaic squares
- Watercolour pencils
- Paintbrushes
- Glue

Approach

1. Stick a border of mosaic squares around each piece of white card.

2. Write a different Roman recipe on each card.

3. Draw a picture in pencil to illustrate each recipe and colour it in using watercolour pencils.

4. Using a paintbrush and water, go over the colouring to transform the work into a painted watercolour.

5. Design a cover for the book with a border of mosaic squares.

6. Gather the loose leaves of the recipe book and display them with food that the Romans ate.

Beliefs

Miwok Creation Story

Native Americans believed that they should live in harmony with the Earth since it provided them with everything they needed in life. They also believed that the sky, plants, birds and animals had their own spirits. They told many different creation stories. One example comes from the Miwok Indians, who told how Coyote created the world and all its creatures:

Resources
- Clay and clay tools
- Garlic press
- Pipe cleaners
- Modelling wire and wire cutters
- Leather scraps
- Beads
- Paint, varnish and paintbrushes

Coyote was worried about who should become the Lord of the Animals. None of the other animals could agree, so Coyote gathered them together and suggested that they all take a lump of clay from the river bed and make a model of the Lord of the Animals – the best one to be chosen as the winner. The animals all began modelling but slept as darkness fell. Coyote, however, stayed awake and continued to work by the light of the moon. When his model was complete he gave it life and before the other animals awoke, a man became the Lord of the Animals.

Approach

1. Model different animals from clay.

2. Put clay into the garlic press to make clay strands to add to the sheep and rams for a woolly coat.

3. Add pipe cleaners to the deer for antlers and curled pipe cleaners for rams' horns.

4. Model a man over a wire armature (framework).

5. Paint all the models and varnish them.

6. Add a costume to the man using leather scraps and beads.

7. Display the man, surrounded by the animals.

Medicine Men

Native Americans had a great belief in healers known as medicine men. Medicine men performed healing rituals including dances, chants and prayers. Navajo healers created large sand paintings on the sick person's floor believing that the sand would absorb the evil sickness. The Tlingit healers used rattles in their healing rituals and Navajo medicine men used snake-shaped prayer sticks to cure stomach problems.

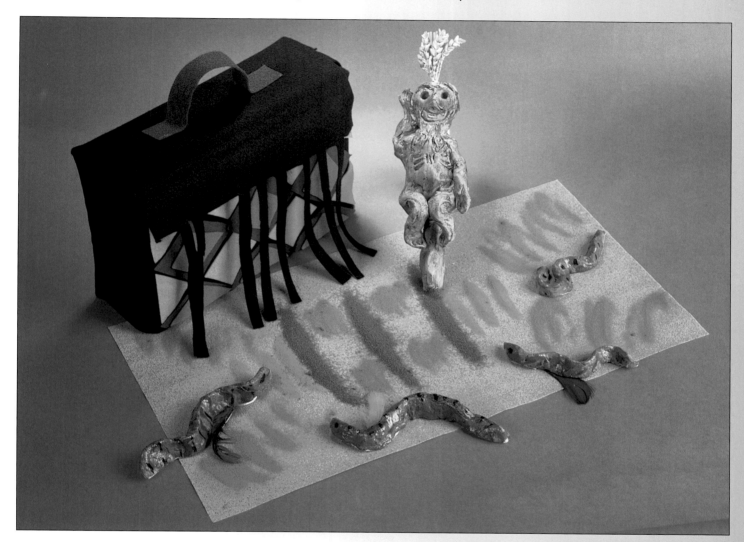

Medicine Bag, Healing Rattle and Prayer Sticks

Resources
- Box
- Orange, yellow, blue and black felt
- Feathers
- Glue
- Clay and clay tools
- Sandpaper
- Fine sand
- Brown shoe polish, cloth and duster
- Powder paints

Approach

1. Cover a box with black felt and glue on geometric shapes in orange, yellow and blue felt.

2. Glue a strip of felt as a handle to the medicine bag.

3. Model a rattle with an exaggerated face out of clay. Allow it to dry and harden.

4. Use a cloth to cover the rattle with brown shoe polish and then shine with a clean duster.

5. Make snake prayer sticks from clay. Add a feather to each finished snake.

6. Display the items on a sand map made by sprinkling sand coloured with powder paints onto a piece of sandpaper.

Childhood and Toys

Relatives or tribal elders would often name a Native American baby instead of the parents. The baby would spend the bulk of its first year strapped into a cradleboard made from beaded cotton tied to a wooden frame. Native Americans hung a beaded pouch in the shape of a lizard or a turtle from the cradleboard, so that their babies would live a long life like those animals.

Cradleboard

Resources
- Balsa wood, sandpaper, silver 3-D paint
- 7–8 tea bags, bowl, hot water
- White cotton fabric
- Shoebox and glue
- Beads, sewing needles and thread
- Fake fur

Approach

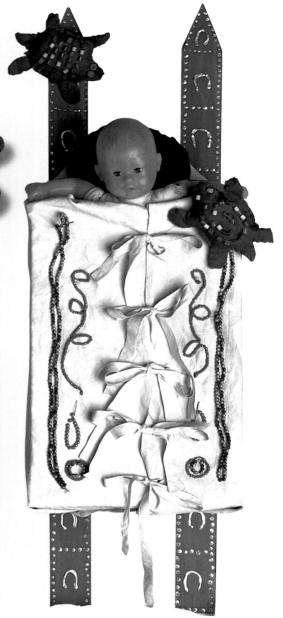

1. Shape two lengths of balsa wood to give pointed ends and sandpaper them for a smooth finish. Paint the wood and decorate it with silver 3-D paint to look like metal studs.

2. Put white cotton fabric into hot water with the tea bags and leave it to soak for two hours. Wring out the fabric and hang out to dry.

3. Cover the shoebox with the dyed fabric so the ends meet over the box opening. With adult supervision, pupils should make holes for fabric ribbons to pass through.

4. Glue the fabric onto the box. Neaten at one end and shape the other end to support the baby's head as shown.

5. Decorate the fabric with beads and add fake fur to support the baby's head and place a doll in the cradleboard.

Turtle Pouch

Resources
- Paper, coloured felt
- Stuffing material
- Beads
- Sewing needles, thread, scissors, pins

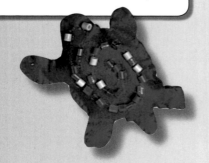

Approach

1. Make a paper pattern for a lizard and a turtle, pin to the felt and cut out two of each shape.

2. Decorate the lizard and the turtle with bead patterns, sewing on the beads with a sewing needle and thread.

3. Sew the two matching felt pieces together, leaving a gap to fill the animal with stuffing.

4. Sew up the gap and hang the pouches from the cradleboard.

Growing up

As children grew up they would gather to listen to stories, which taught them about their tribal history and their customs. Girls would learn to sew, weave baskets, embroider, tan hides and cook. They would play with miniature tepees, cradleboards and dolls. Boys would learn how to make and use bows and arrows and how to hunt and fight. Their first buffalo kill was an important event celebrated with presents and a feast.

Toy Cradleboards

Resources
- Matchboxes
- Lolly sticks
- Felt
- Beads
- Felt-tipped pens
- Glue

Approach

1. Cover a slightly open matchbox with felt and decorate it with beads.

2. Glue the matchbox to two lolly sticks, which make the wooden frame and can be decorated with felt-tipped pen.

Miniature Tepees

Resources
- White or cream cotton fabric
- Fabric crayons
- Pins
- Gardening or barbeque sticks
- String
- Glue

Approach

1. Photocopy the tepee template on page 72. Cut it out to use as a paper pattern.

2. Cut the tepee shape out of fabric and decorate with Indian designs using fabric crayons.

3. Tie four sticks together as the framework of the tepee and put the fabric around the frame, gluing it into place.

4. Display with the toy cradle boards.

Games and Sports

Many tribes played team sports such as lacrosse, stickball and kickball, which could be fast, rather violent games. Other popular sports were canoeing, horse racing and archery. A hoop and pole game, where a lance had to be thrown through a rolling hoop, was very popular, as were card and gambling games. Bets would be made on dice that had been carved and painted with spiders, lizards and turtles. Packs of cards were cut from rawhide and painted with designs.

Hoop and Pole Game

Make decorated hoops and lances for the hoop and pole game and try it out in the playground under supervision.

Resources
- Wire and wire cutters
- Beads
- Raffia
- Bamboo poles or wooden dowelling
- Feathers

Approach

1. Make a small circle of wire, threaded with beads, for the centre of the hoop.

2. Cut four lengths of wire approximately 4cm in length and attach each one to the small circle of wire, spaced evenly.

3. Thread beads onto each piece of wire and join them to a larger outer ring of wire.

4. Attach a further outer ring to the first with wire and wind coloured raffia around them.

5. Decorate the end of each bamboo pole with feathers to make a lance.

Playing Cards

Resources
- Leather and coloured card
- Felt-tipped pens

Approach

1. Make a card template.

2. Cut the cards from pieces of leather or coloured card.

3. Use felt-tipped pens to draw different Native American symbols on each card and devise your own games.

Clothing

Many Native American men wore shirts, tunics, leggings, loincloths and belts all made from leather. Women wore skirts or dresses, adding shawls for extra warmth. Animal skins were stretched out on the ground so that any flesh or fur could be scraped off. The skins were rubbed with a special paste to make them soft and stop them from rotting.

The clothes were painted or printed with patterns and then decorated with porcupine quills, beads and horsehair tassels. The women took great pride in their skills with quills, which would be dyed and flattened before being sewn on with sinew. Porcupine quills would also be used to decorate their leather shoes known as moccasins.

Plains Indian Shirt

Resources
- White cotton fabric
- 7–8 tea bags, bowl, hot water
- Cocktail sticks, blue, red and green food colouring
- Plasticine, clay tools
- Paints and paintbrushes
- Newspaper, pins
- Sewing needles and thread
- Beads

Approach

1. Draw and colour some shirt designs on paper.

2. Dye the cotton fabric in a bowl of hot water with the tea bags. Leave the material to soak for two hours and then hang it out to dry.

3. Put the cocktail sticks into food colouring to dye for 30–60 minutes and then spread them on newspaper to dry.

4. Make a cube from plasticine as a printing block. Press the clay tools into the plasticine to make a Native American design.

5. Make a paper pattern for the shirt out of newspaper and pin to the dyed cotton material. Cut out a front and a back.

6. Sew the shirt together and then, with newspaper flat inside the middle of the shirt, print the design using the plasticine block. Thread beads onto the dyed cocktail sticks and add to the costume.

7. Make even cuts at the bottom of the shirt to create a fringed effect.

Ceremonies and Rituals

Native Americans dressed up in ceremonial clothing to celebrate many different events throughout their lives. Marriage ceremonies varied greatly between different tribes. The Hopi tribe sealed their marriage partnership by having their hair washed together in one bowl. On the wedding day the Hopi girl would have an elaborate hairstyle and the boy would wear several bead necklaces. Menominee newly-weds would receive a pair of dolls to help them have a long and happy marriage. These 'love dolls' would be tied face-to-face to ensure the couple were faithful to each other.

Menominee Love Dolls

Resources
- Wooden spoons
- Paints and paintbrushes
- Fabric scraps
- Beads
- String
- Wool

Approach

1. Paint a spoon as the face of a Menominee Indian and add wool for hair.

2. Wrap the spoon in fabric to represent clothes. Add some beading to the material.

3. Tie two dolls together with string, face-to-face or side-by-side, to represent the couple having a long and happy marriage.

Sun Mask

The Native Americans had ceremonies to dance or pray for good harvests, health and successful hunting. Many tribes performed versions of the sun dance as an offering to the Great Spirit. The dancers, all male, would leap in a huge circle around a tall pole, copying the sun moving across the sky. Dance hoops were shaken and music was played on drums decorated with moons and suns. Dancers wore spectacular carved masks to enhance the story they were telling. A sun mask was worn during winter ceremonies. It had four oval faces and upraised hands surrounding a central face that represented the Spirit of the Sun.

Approach

1. Cut out a large cardboard oval, then draw and cut out four small pumpkin-shaped faces, four hand shapes and one large disc for the central symbol of the sun.

2. Glue all the cut-out shapes on the large cardboard oval as shown. Add cut-out cardboard eyes, eyebrows, lips and a nose to the central symbol, gluing them in place.

3. Spread the whole sun mask in glue and cover it with torn-up strips of white tissue paper. Allow it to dry.

4. Add wax crayon designs to the hands and faces. Paint over the wax crayons for a resist effect and varnish the sun mask when dry.

Resources
- Cardboard, glue
- Masking tape
- White tissue paper
- Paints and paintbrushes
- Wax crayons
- Varnish

Drums and Drumsticks

Resources
- Biscuit tins and cardboard tubs
- Cream calico fabric, fabric crayons
- Modroc plaster bandages
- Paints and paintbrushes
- Wool, large sewing needles
- Wooden spoons
- Large pebbles

Approach

1. Cut the calico fabric into circles slightly larger than the tops and bottoms of the different tubs and tins. A Native American design can be drawn on the fabric to decorate, if desired, using fabric crayons.

2. Soak strips of modroc in water for 3–4 seconds and cover the tubs and tins. When the modroc is dry and hard, paint designs onto the tubs and tins.

3. Add a fabric circle to the top and bottom of each drum and sew in place using a needle threaded with wool.

4. Wrap a pebble and spoon in calico and tie securely using the wool. Display the drums and drumsticks with the sun mask.

Beliefs and Legends

Australian Aborigines believe that their Ancestors lived under the ground before the world was made. In 'Dreamtime' the Ancestors awoke and walked all over the empty land singing of birds and trees, rocks and mountains and as they sang the world was created. When their task was finished the Ancestors went back to sleep. The Australian Aborigines had, and still have, many ceremonies and traditions linked to Dreamtime.

The Binbinga tribe tell a story about a snake spirit, Bobbi-bobbi, who lived on Earth during Dreamtime. Bobbi-bobbi sent some fruit-eating bats for men to eat but they flew too high for them to catch. To solve the problem Bobbi-bobbi pulled out one of his ribs and threw it to the men below. Bobbi-bobbi told them if they used it to catch the bats by throwing it through the air it would go back to them. This is how the boomerang came to be used as a hunting tool.

Boomerang Designs

Resources
● Cardboard
● Oil pastels
● Clay tools or paintbrush handles

Approach

1. Cut out a boomerang shape from cardboard.

2. Cover the boomerang with oil pastels in different colours.

3. Scratch designs into the waxy oil pastels using a small sharp tool such as a pointed clay tool or the end of a wooden paintbrush to create distinct patterns and textures.

The Rainbow Bird Story

The Australian Aborigines also told a story about 'The Rainbow Bird' to explain how fire came to be used for warmth and light:

In the very beginning there was Crocodile Man and Crocodile Man was the only one to have fire. He could breathe fire or hold it on a stick with his foot or balance it on his head to show off to the other animals. The other creatures wanted fire to keep them warm or give them light but Crocodile Man was mean and selfish and would not share it.

Birdwoman lived in the trees near Crocodile Man and she longed to have fire for warmth and to cook the small reptiles and fish that she ate raw each day. She often flew down to Crocodile Man to beg him for his fire stick but he would not give it away. Birdwoman did not give up waiting and one day her chance came. She sat in a tree and watched Crocodile Man yawning again and again until he finally fell asleep. Birdwoman flew down and grabbed the fire stick in her claws and flew away as quickly as she could. Birdwoman was not selfish like Crocodile Man and she decided to share her good fortune with everybody. She flew in spirals around the forest to put fire into the heart of every tree. This enabled mankind to make fire using twigs and branches to cook their food, keep warm and to light their way.

Birdwoman was transformed into a beautiful rainbow bird after her generosity. Rainbow Bird flew back to Crocodile Man and taunted him, saying that she had the freedom of the air whilst he would spend the remainder of his days in the swamps. Rainbow Bird flew off displaying her beautiful colours.

Rainbow Bird Wall Hanging

Resources
- Thin paper
- Individual cotton squares
- Pins
- Coloured felt
- Sewing needles and thread or glue
- Backing material

Approach

1. Design appliqué squares to tell the story of 'The Rainbow Bird'. Draw the designs on paper the same size as the cotton squares.

2. Cut out the designs and use them as paper patterns. Pin the paper patterns to felt and cut out the shapes.

3. Sew or glue the felt shapes onto the cotton squares.

4. Assemble the story squares to make a large wall hanging, either gluing or sewing each square onto the backing material.

Ceremonies and Rituals

The Australian Aborigines had, and continue to celebrate, many ceremonies that link them with their Ancestors and their belief in Dreamtime. The Ancestors gave them laws about living together harmoniously and how to live from the land without harming it. Aboriginal art was mostly linked with Dreamtime ceremonies. People, their spirits and animals were painted onto rocks, bark and stones. Aborigines in central Australia often drew maps in the sand to explain how different Ancestors made different parts of the land. The maps showed in dots and lines the footsteps the Ancestors took when creating the land and from these sand paintings a new style of Aboriginal art evolved. Modern Aboriginal artists have used and developed this distinctive, dotted style on canvas. The dotted patterns now feature as decoration on many souvenirs from Australia.

Bark and Stone Paintings

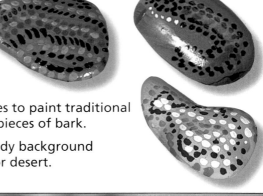

Resources
- Pebbles
- Pieces of bark
- Paint
- Paintbrushes

Approach

1. Use the wooden end of the paintbrushes to paint traditional dot patterns onto the pebbles and the pieces of bark.

2. Display the artwork with logs and a sandy background reminiscent of the Australian outback or desert.

Mirror Frames

Explore the dot painting style by creating patterned mirror frames.

Resources
- Mirror tiles
- Wooden or cardboard frames
- Paints
- Paintbrushes

Approach

1. Glue a mirror tile into the middle of the wooden or cardboard frame.

2. Use the wooden end of a paintbrush to paint traditional dot patterns onto the frame.

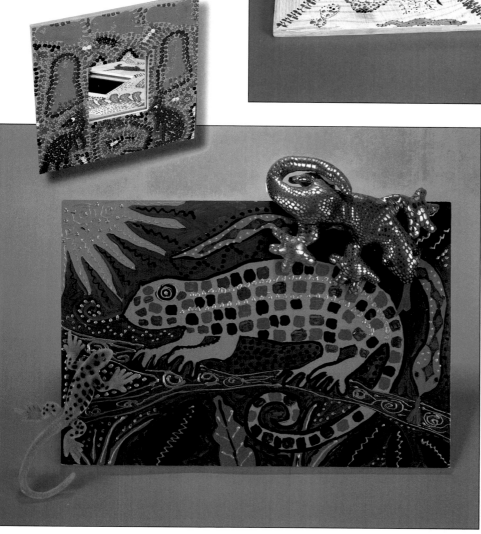

Acrylic Paintings

Resources
- Small pieces of hardboard
- Acrylic paints
- 3-D paints
- Paintbrushes

Approach

1. Draw an Australian animal on a piece of hardboard.

2. Paint the picture using bold acrylic paints and leave it to dry.

3. Cover the painting with the traditional dot patterns using 3-D paints.

Bubble-wrap Printing

Resources
- Bubble-wrap
- Paints and paintbrushes
- Large sheets of white or coloured paper

Approach

1. Paint the raised bubbles of the bubble-wrap to show patterned animals, flowers, plants and so on.

2. When the bubble-wrap is completely covered, and still wet, turn it over and print the design onto a large sheet of paper.

Aboriginal-style Mobile

Resources
- Wire coat hangers
- Sandpaper
- Paints and paintbrushes
- Wool or string
- Masking tape

Approach

1. Bend a coat hanger into a fish shape.

2. Draw around the fish shape onto sandpaper and cut the shape out.

3. Draw small Australian animals in pencil on the back of some more sandpaper and cut them out.

4. Dip the end of a paintbrush in paint and decorate each animal and the large fish with traditional Aboriginal dot patterns.

5. Use masking tape to stick the fish onto the hanger, then hang lengths of wool or string from the back of the fish and attach the smaller animals to them.

Homes and Family

In ancient times, Australian Aborigines lived in rural environments. They believed that the Ancestors created the land and that it should be well cared for. Aborigines, who lived a nomadic life, would sometimes stay six months in one place, sometimes only a week. It often depended on how much food there was for them to gather. Camps were quickly set up, with huts of stick and bark or grass shelters. Each tribe would have its own name and its own language.

Today Australian Aborigines are a kind and caring people who look after their close family and their wider extended family or tribe. They are a proud people who have had to fight for their rights and to keep the identity that is so fundamental to their beliefs. The red on their flag symbolizes the Aboriginal blood spilled over the many years since the British colonized Australia, the gold is the sun and the black represents the Aboriginal people.

Aboriginal Flag Design

Resources
- Coloured felt
- Glue
- Wooden dowelling
- Hole punch
- 3-D paints

Approach

1. Sketch ideas for the flag that symbolize the Aboriginal way of life.

2. Select the most interesting ideas and put them together in a single class design.

3. Cut out the shapes from coloured felt and glue them onto the background, which should be in the colours of the present Aborigine flag – black, yellow and red felt.

4. Any designs drawn in the traditional dotted pattern can be made by punching the dots from felt using a hole punch and gluing them to the fabric.

5. Add further decoration, using 3-D paints.

6. Hang the flag from a piece of dowelling.

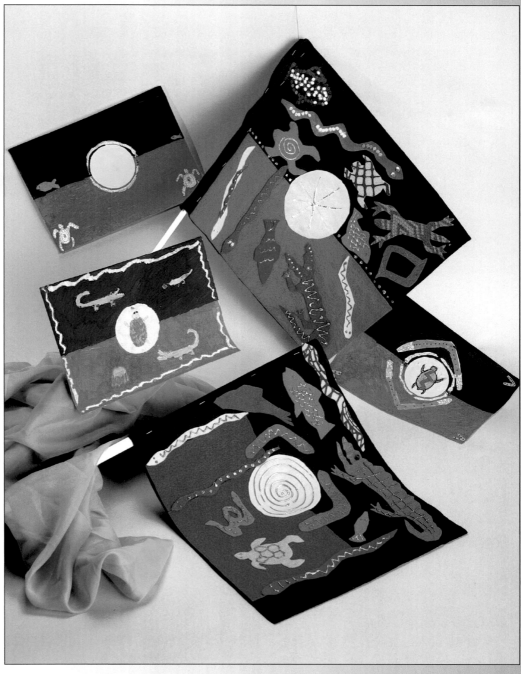

Beliefs

It was nearly 5000 years ago that a civilisation grew up around the Indus River in Asia. Many great cities were built where artistic and religious life was rich and varied. Hinduism and Buddhism were two of the religions that developed in tandem with this civilisation. Ancient Indians were inspired by their religious beliefs to build wonderful temples and palaces and to create beautiful sculptures.

Over the centuries, India has been invaded many times. The first invaders were the Aryans who divided society into three classes (castes), which were priests (Brahmin), warriors (Kshatviya) and property holders (Vaishya). A group of labourers and servants constituted a fourth caste. Only the highest born Brahmins could be saved from life's suffering which the other castes began to think was unjust.

A man called Siddhartha Gautama, who became known as the Buddha, taught a 'middle way' which people of any caste could follow – and the Buddhist way of life was established. Symbols of the Buddha's life were the Bodhi tree, where he meditated and gained enlightenment, and footprints covered in signs to stand for his continued presence.

In AD 200 the Aryan religion evolved into Hinduism. Hindus believe in one Supreme Being, Brahman the high god, who takes on three main forms – Brahma the Creator, Vishnu the Preserver and Shiva the Destroyer.

Brahma, Shiva and Vishnu Paintings

Resources
- Oil pastels
- Thin cardboard
- Drawing inks
- Paintbrushes
- Masking tape
- Gold doilies

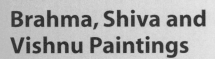

Approach

1. Draw a picture of Buddha, Brahma, Shiva or Vishnu and colour using oil pastels.

2. Paint over chosen areas of the pictures with drawing inks.

3. Make a frame for each picture using gold doilies and use masking tape to stick them in place.

Legends

The hero of many Indian stories is Mahavira, who appeared on Earth to save the world. He is also one of the key figures in the religion, Jainism. Queen Trishala, Mahavira's earthly mother, had many dreams about how great her son would be and what he would achieve. In a succession of dreams, she saw a huge, white elephant with four gold tusks, a noble bull and a lion, the Sun and Moon, a lotus pond and an ocean of milk. When his earthly parents died, Mahavira left his wife and baby daughter to find the meaning of life. After many years of self-denial and meditation, the meaning of life became clear to him. He spent the rest of his life travelling through India spreading his message. When his life on Earth ended he returned to heaven to sit above his people on a shining throne made of stars and diamonds.

Silk Dream Paintings

Approach

1. Draw a design depicting one of Mahavira's mother's dreams in pencil on white paper. Go over the design in black felt-tipped pen.

2. Cut the silk into squares slightly larger than the wooden frames.

3. Stretch the silk over the wooden frame, pinning on opposite sides to make the silk taut.

4. Put the design under the frame and then copy the outline onto the silk material with the gutta outliner. Leave to dry.

5. Paint inside the gutta outlines with coloured silk paints. Use water to clean the brushes.

Resources
- Simple wooden frames
- Silk, silk paints and paintbrushes
- Silk outliner pens (gutta) in gold and black
- Silk painting pins
- Masking tape
- Sequins and jewels
- Cardboard frames
- 3-D paints, felt-tipped pens

6. When the silk paints are dry, add more details with the gutta outliners.

7. Decorate the cardboard frames using felt-tipped pens, jewels, sequins and 3-D paints.

8. Mount the silk painting in the cardboard frame with masking tape and place on display.

Festivals and Ceremonies

In ancient times, there were many important Hindu festivals and ceremonies held throughout the year. Many of these festivals are still celebrated in the Hindu world today. People would dress in their best clothes and celebrate with parades, singing and dancing. The nine nights leading up to the festival of Dussehra are known as Navratri. A special shrine is built in the temple and women in beautiful saris dance around the shrine with sticks that symbolize sickles, as this was originally a harvest celebration. Worship is offered to the goddess Devi in all her different forms. The story of Rama's search for his kidnapped wife, Sita, is told and the story ends when Rama kills the ten-headed Demon King, Ravana, and Sita is free.

Demon King Ravana

Resources

- Large cardboard tube
- Two smaller cardboard tubes
- Two cardboard tubs
- Round box
- Modroc plaster bandages
- Paints and paintbrushes
- Ribbon
- 3-D paints
- Black sugar paper
- Miniature toy figures
- Glue

Approach

1. Cover the round box for the head and two joined tubs for the upper body with modroc strips, soaked in water for 3–4 seconds.

2. Add two smaller tubes to the upper body and shape as arms. Soak modroc strips in water for 3–4 seconds before covering the body. Allow to dry.

3. Paint the round box white and then paint on Ravana's ten heads.

4. Paint the large cardboard tube and the upper body with black paint. Glue the upper body onto the large tube.

5. Shape black sugar paper around the large tube as Ravana's clothing and decorate with 3-D paints and ribbon.

6. Display the model with miniature toy people to show the scale of the colossal effigies that are used in the Dussehra festival.

Dussehra Elephants

Many religious traditions that were started by the Ancient Indians persist to this day. In the state of Mysore the festival of Dussehra is still celebrated with a parade of beautifully decorated elephants through the streets.

Approach

Resources
- Clay and clay tools
- Mirror mosaics
- Beads and jewels
- Coloured braid
- Cocktail umbrellas

1. Model an elephant from clay, moulding or pulling the legs and trunk out from the body of the elephant rather than joining them on.

2. Add braid to the top of the elephant's head and push in beads for eyes.

3. Push beads, jewels and mosaic glass into the clay to decorate the elephant.

4. If you model riders for the elephants, give them cocktail umbrellas for the brightly-coloured sunshades that the riders carry during the festival.

Rangoli Patterns

Diwali, known as the festival of lights, was also celebrated in Ancient India. Once again Rama and Sita were remembered – this time for their return home to their kingdom after 14 years in exile. Clay lamps were put on doorsteps where beautiful Rangoli patterns were made using rice or coloured powders to welcome visitors. The goddess of wealth and prosperity, Lakshmi, was also worshipped as the people hoped for good fortune in the year ahead.

Resources
- Fine sand, salt or rice
- Small containers
- Powder paints in several bright colours
- Hardboard
- Paintbrushes
- Gold and silver 3-D paints
- Glue

Approach

1. Design a Rangoli pattern and draw it on a piece of hardboard in pencil.

2. Go over the outlines of the design in silver or gold 3-D paint and leave it to dry and harden.

3. Put the sand, salt or rice into small containers and mix with coloured powder paints.

4. Cover areas of the design with glue and then sprinkle on the coloured sand, salt or rice, until the design is complete.

Wesak Cards

Buddhist festivals were times to remember the Buddha's teachings. Wesak, the most important Buddhist festival today, was also celebrated in ancient times. At Wesak, Buddhists celebrate Buddha's birthday. It is held on the day of the full moon in May or June. At Wesak, Buddhists would decorate their homes with flowers and lamps. Today, Buddhists give cards and small gifts such as incense sticks, candles or flowers.

Resources
- Oil pastels
- Gold 3-D paint
- Corrugated card or plain coloured card
- A4 thin white card

Approach

1. Draw different Buddhist designs on white A4 card.

2. Colour in the designs using oil pastels.

3. Use gold 3-D paint to outline some of the images.

4. Mount the finished designs onto folded plain or corrugated card.

Transport and Travel

Travelling on foot was the most common way of getting about in Ancient India. Horses, oxen, camels and elephants carried heavy loads. Camels were used for transport in hot, dry regions as they could travel for long periods without water. Boats, steered with a large oar, were used to travel along rivers in the north of India. For nearly 5000 years, carts pulled by bullocks or cows have been the main form of long-distance transport. Emperors would sometimes travel in an elaborate chair carried on the shoulders of servants. This was known as a palanquin. Emperors could also ride in style on top of an elephant, a symbol of royalty. Attendants and courtiers would follow the procession.

Lino Prints

Resources
- Lino blocks
- Lino cutting tools
- Printing inks
- Rollers and trays
- White paper

Approach

1. Draw a design in pencil on the lino showing a form of travel used in Ancient India. Work on one large piece of lino divided into quarters or four small, individual squares.

2. Working in small groups under close adult supervision, use the lino cutting tools to cut away the areas of lino that are not to be printed. The raised areas of lino will make the print.

3. Put printing ink into a tray and roll a printing roller back and forth so that it is covered with ink.

4. Roll the roller across the lino block or one quarter of the lino block. If the design is divided into four pictures, use four different colours for printing. Make sure colours do not overlap, or allow them to dry between printing.

5. Put paper on top of the lino block and, with a clean roller, roll over the paper in different directions. A border can be added using a design made on a smaller square of lino.

Clothing and Jewellery

Print Block Clothing

Resources
- Small wooden blocks
- Coloured foam
- Glue, paints and paintbrushes
- Cardboard
- Cotton or silk fabric

The textile trade has always been important in India. Silk was first brought to India from China along the Silk Road but from about AD 100 India produced its own silk and exported it to other countries. Dyes were made from various plants and vegetables and the silk was dyed in plain, bright colours. Turkish and Persian invaders introduced floral designs in about AD 110. Traditional wooden printing blocks were used and are still used in the production of colourful fabrics today.

In Ancient India many clothes were draped and folded rather than sewn. Hindu men wore garments called dhotis, whilst the single piece of fabric wrapped around the body by the women became the sari. Both men and women wore lots of jewellery – earrings, nose-rings, armbands and anklets.

Approach

1. Draw figures onto a piece of cardboard and paint the faces, arms and legs.

2. Draw an Indian-inspired pattern shape on a piece of foam or cardboard, cut it out and then glue it onto a wooden block. Leave it to dry.

3. Using a paintbrush, paint the raised shape on the printing block and print the shape onto the fabric. Repeat until the material is covered.

4. Cut the fabric to make a costume for the figure or wind the material around the figure for a sari.

Storytelling

For many centuries, tales of folklore and stories about the gods were passed down by word of mouth before eventually being written down. The kavad is a storehouse of tales, which represents the ancient tradition of telling stories through pictures. A latch on the storyteller's stomach can be undone to reveal beautiful paintings telling a story on the opening hinged doors and in the box itself.

Make a story-box and a set of miniature books as a class project. Tell the stories of Brahma, Vishnu and Shiva as well as other Indian tales.

Resources
- Shoebox
- Cardboard and corrugated card
- Masking tape
- Paints and paintbrushes
- Watercolour pencils
- Paper for miniature books
- Glue

Approach

1. Make folding doors from corrugated card and stick them to the shoebox with masking tape.

2. Make a head from cardboard, decorate it and tape it to the top of the shoebox.

3. Illustrate an Indian story on small pieces of white paper using watercolour pencils to colour the illustrations.

4. Transform the pictures into miniature watercolour paintings by painting over with a brush and water.

5. Glue the miniature paintings on the inside of the story-box and its doors.

6. Illustrate other Indian stories in miniature storybooks.

Beliefs

The Vikings were brave warriors and explorers from Norway, Sweden and Denmark. They believed in many different gods and goddesses. The chief gods were Odin, Thor, Frey and Freyja. Odin was the god of wisdom and war. The greatest honour for a Viking warrior was to die in battle. According to legend, Odin had a group of female attendants, known as Valkyries, who flew over battlefields taking the souls of dead warriors. The souls were taken to Odin's palace, Valhalla, that had walls made of shields and rafters made of spears. The palace was also said to have hundreds of doors. The warriors improved their fighting skills by day and feasted all night waiting for Ragnarok, a great battle that would signal the end of the world.

Odin Mobile

Make a mobile with Odin's palace and the Valkyries carrying the warriors up to Valhalla.

Resources
- Clothes drying hoop with hanging pegs
- Thin cardboard
- Watercolour pencils
- Masking tape and wool

Approach

1. Fold a rectangle of cardboard into a circle that fits on top of the drying hoop.

2. Flatten out the card and draw Odin's palace, Valhalla, that had rafters made of spears, walls made of shields and hundreds of doors.

3. Draw Odin standing in one of the doors.

4. On another piece of card, draw Valkyries carrying the dead warriors and cut them out.

5. Colour the palace, Odin and the Valkyries using watercolour pencils. Using water, paint over the colouring to achieve a painted watercolour effect.

6. Attach the palace to the drying hoop. Hang the Valkyries and the warriors from the hoop using the hanging pegs and wool or string.

Blazing Funeral Pyre

The Vikings buried their loved ones with everything that they would need in the next life. Wealthy Vikings were often buried in boats full of their belongings and sometimes even with their servants. The ships were buried in mounds or set alight and pushed out to sea in a blazing funeral pyre. The Vikings believed that the ship with its occupant sailed off to Asgard, the land of the Norse gods. Some people set up stones in memory of their dead relatives, which had pictures or inscriptions on them. Some of the pictures were carved and then painted. Poor people were buried in holes in the ground in hollowed-out tree trunks. They would be dressed in their best clothes with a few possessions such as a comb, some bobbins and wool for spinning, and a barrel of milk.

Approach

1. Draw the longship and lots of leaping flames.

2. Colour the picture using wax crayons, pressing down heavily to make the colours thick and bold.

3. Carefully screw up the picture to crack the wax and then flatten it out by hand.

4. Paint over the picture using drawing inks.

5. When dry, iron the painting between sheets of white sugar paper.

Resources
- White paper
- White sugar paper
- Wax crayons
- Drawing inks, paintbrushes
- An iron

 Note: An adult should use the iron at all times.

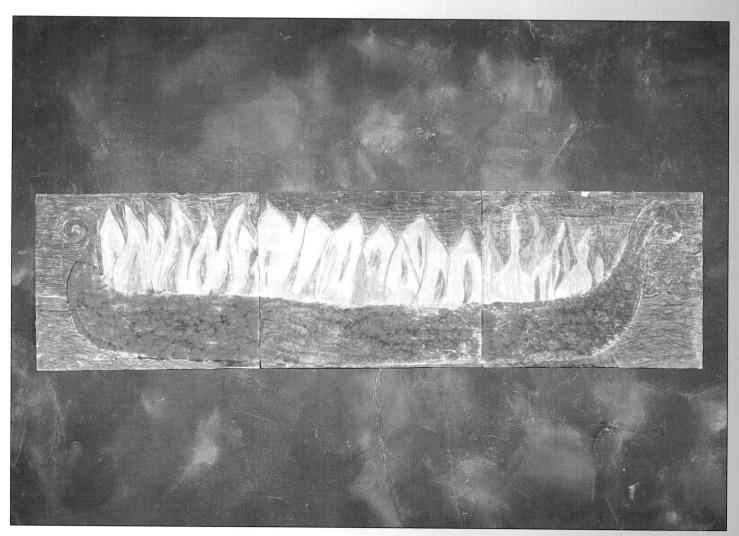

Viking Runic Stone

The Viking system of writing was made up of marks or letters called runes. As the Vikings did not have paper or pens they carved their runes into wood, bones or stone. The Viking alphabet was called the futhark after the sounds of the first six runes. There were 16 runes altogether. The Vikings erected stone monuments to their dead relatives. Some had pictures carved on them which were then painted.

Resources
- Stones
- Clay tools
- Paints
- Paintbrushes

Approach

1. Draw a design on a stone with a soft pencil.

2. Paint the design.

3. Add a runic inscription by scraping away the wet paint with clay tools.

Legends

The Vikings told many stories about the next world. If the person had lived a good life they would go to the hall of gods and goddesses in Asgard. Leading a bad life would mean being taken to the land of the dead ruled by the goddess, Hel. Hel had a beautiful face and upper body but from the waist downwards she was a hideous skeleton. Her home, Eljundir, was guarded by a fierce dog, making sure that those who entered never left.

Goddess Hel Paintings

Resources
- White and black paper
- White paint
- Paintbrushes
- Watercolour pencils

Approach

1. Draw pictures of Hel and her dog with a suitable background.

2. Colour the work using watercolour pencils.

3. Using a paintbrush, paint over the colours with water to achieve a painted watercolour effect.

4. Draw arm and leg shapes on black paper and cut them out.

5. Paint white bones onto the cut-out shapes and use them to make a frame around the painting.

Hel Puppets

Resources
- White and black paper
- White paint, paintbrushes
- Felt-tipped pens
- Masking tape, glue
- Shiny fabric
- Wooden sticks

Approach

1. Draw Hel's upper body and head on white paper and colour with felt-tipped pens.

2. Draw Hel's legs on black paper and paint the bones in white paint.

3. Join the legs onto the body with masking tape.

4. Add a skirt made from shiny fabric.

5. Use masking tape to attach a stick onto the back of the body.

Clothing and Jewellery

To the Vikings, warmth and comfort were more important than style, and clothes were often worn in layers to keep out the cold. Men wore knee-length tunics with woollen leggings and a woollen cape (held together with a decorative brooch if he was a nobleman). The tunics were often decorated at the cuffs, hem and neckline with bright woven braids of patterned cloth. Leather belts were worn to keep up trousers and support weapons. Linen was used for undergarments and cloth would be coloured with vegetable dyes. Woollen tunics were often woven with a checked or other geometric pattern.

Women wore ankle-length dresses often with a pinafore over the top. Some women wore chains hanging from their tunic brooches from which they hung a comb, keys or scissors. Viking clothing did not have any pockets. They wore headbands or linen bonnets and fur-lined hats in the winter. Shoes and boots were made from leather and fastened with a strap and toggle or could be slipped on with no fastening. We know about the clothes that the Vikings wore from embroideries, tapestries and pictures carved on stone monuments. Both men and women loved to wear decorative jewellery and the Vikings were very skilled metalworkers.

Dough Figures

Resources
- Plain flour and salt
- Mixing bowl and spoon
- Garlic press
- Non-stick baking tray
- Paints, varnish and paintbrushes
- Woollen and linen fabric
- Sewing thread and needles
- Leather scraps
- Decorative buttons, ribbon

Approach

1. Make up salt dough using a mixture of two cups of flour to every cup of salt used.

2. Add water to the mixture until it makes a soft, pliable dough – not too dry and not too sticky.

3. Using a hand-sized ball of dough, model the head and body of a Viking figure and then add arms and legs, joining with water.

4. Add hair, and beards for the men, by squeezing dough through a garlic press. (Vikings often braided their beards or parted them in the middle.)

5. Bake the dough models on a non-stick baking tray in the oven at 150°C (300°F, Gas Mark 2) for 3–4 hours. Leave them to cool in the oven.

6. Paint the figures and varnish them.

7. Make typical Viking costumes for the models. Sew or glue them onto the figures. Add decorative buttons to fasten garments.

Food and Farming

Most Vikings lived by farming and small communities grew up where the soil was good for growing crops. Spring and autumn were busy times of the year with planting and harvesting but in summer, the men often went on hunting or raiding expeditions. The farmer's wife would milk the cows and sheep to make butter and cheese. She would also carry the house keys and be in charge of the household finances.

The Vikings ate lots of stewed meat that was cooked in iron cauldrons. For Vikings who lived near the coast, fish was the staple diet. Cod, herring, haddock and eels were all caught and eaten. Fish and meat were hung in the wind to dry or pickled in salt water so that they would have a supply of food throughout the winter. Garlic and onions were added to stews. Cabbages and peas were common vegetables. Viking settlers on the Atlantic islands ate roasted seagulls and poached seagull eggs. There was plenty of fruit to pick and eat in the forests, such as blackberries, raspberries and plums.

Resources
- Plain flour and salt
- Mixing bowl and spoon
- Non-stick baking tray
- Paints, varnish and paintbrushes
- Wire and wire cutters
- Wood-effect wallpaper or wrapping paper and twigs

Viking Kitchen

Approach

1. Make up salt dough using a mixture of two cups of flour to every cup of salt used.

2. Slowly add water to the mixture until it makes a soft, pliable dough.

3. Model an open fireplace, iron pots, a cauldron, wooden bowls, bowls of vegetables and eggs, drinking horns, jugs, a griddle for baking bread and a quern for grinding grain. (A quern was made from two circular stones placed one on top of the other.) Add a wire handle to the cauldron.

4. Bake the kitchen items on a non-stick baking tray in the oven at 150°C (300°F, Gas Mark 2) for $1\frac{1}{2}$–2 hours. Leave the dough models to cool in the oven.

5. Paint and varnish the models.

6. Add some twigs to the open fireplace and put the cauldron on the fire. Add some wood-effect wallpaper or wrapping paper as the walls or flooring.

Transport and Travel

The Vikings used two main types of boat – longships for raids and war and knarrs for fishing and trading – both propelled by oars and a central square sail. The sails were often dyed blood red to strike fear into those they were sailing to attack. The boats were built from fir, pine or oak and decorated with menacing figureheads to frighten their enemies or to protect the sailors from evil. The figures were usually mythical monsters, the dragon being a great favourite. Their shields slotted into a shield rack that ran along the side of the boat. Shields were often covered in leather or painted in bright colours. The shields could be pulled out of the rack when they fought at sea or on the shore.

Viking Ships

Resources
- Brown plasticine
- Gardening sticks
- Red corrugated card
- Rubber washers
- Silk painting pins
- Thin card
- Glue

Approach

1. Use strips of plasticine to make the wooden sides of the boat, then model a figurehead and add a bottom to the boat.

2. Put silk painting pins into the middle of the rubber washers and push them into the plasticine along the top of the boat to represent shields.

3. Cut out a sail shape from red corrugated card and glue it onto one of the gardening sticks. Fix the stick into the base of the boat.

4. Make oars from thin card and glue them to the sticks. Push the sticks through the plasticine between each of the shields.

5. Display the boat (or boats) with a seascape or shoreline foreground.

Viking Weather Vane

The Vikings were excellent sailors. Whenever possible they kept in sight of land, but when far out to sea they navigated by the sun and stars, using their great knowledge of seabirds and wind and wave patterns. Weather vanes, decorated with lions and birds, were used to tell the direction of the wind. They were hung from the prow or mast of a Viking ship.

Approach

1. Cut the black card into a weather vane shape.

2. Decorate the weather vane with dragons, lions or birds using the 3-D paints.

3. Cut out an animal shape from black card and glue it to the top of the weather vane. Decorate the animal using the 3-D paints.

Resources
- Black card
- Gold and silver 3-D paints
- Glue

Tepee Template

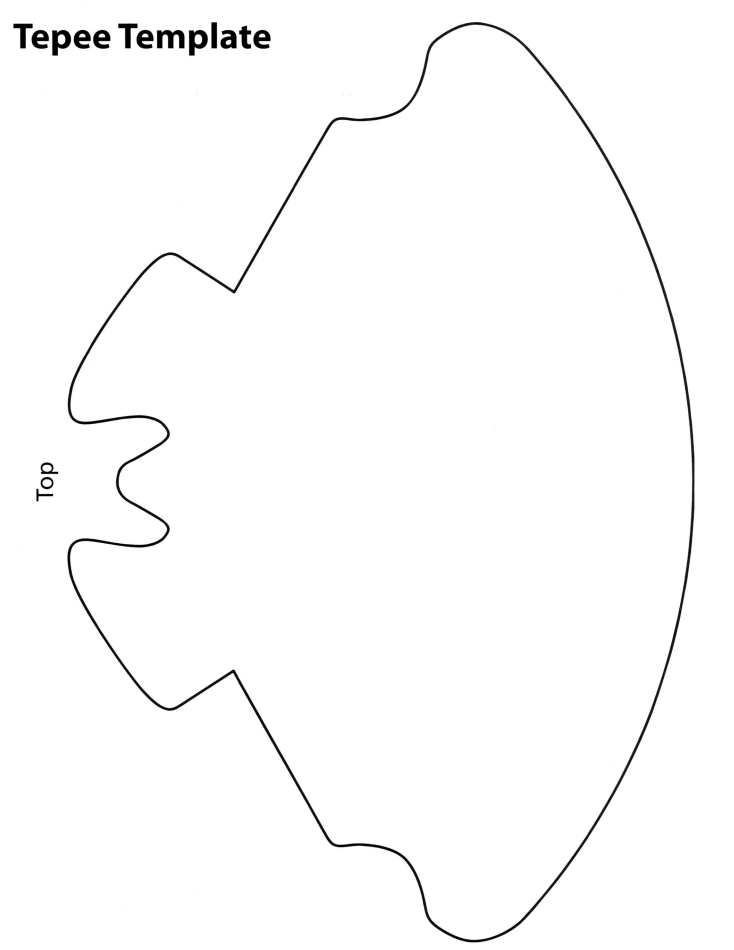

Top